AF270503

THE HAUNTED HISTORY OF
SALEM, MASSACHUSETTS

BY TAMMY GAGNE

Cover image: The haunted people executed during the Salem witch trials were originally buried in shallow graves near where they hanged. Historians believe those executed were later reburied in another location by their families.

An Imprint of Abdo Publishing
abdobooks.com

abdobooks.com

Published by Abdo Publishing, a division of ABDO, PO Box 398166, Minneapolis, Minnesota 55439. Copyright © 2024 by Abdo Consulting Group, Inc. International copyrights reserved in all countries. No part of this book may be reproduced in any form without written permission from the publisher. Core Library™ is a trademark and logo of Abdo Publishing.

Printed in the United States of America, North Mankato, Minnesota.
102023
012024

Cover Photo: Shutterstock Images
Interior Photos: Wangkun Jia/Shutterstock Images, 4–5; mikroman6/Moment/Getty Images, 6; Stan Tess/Alamy, 9; Everett Collection/Shutterstock Images, 10, 14–15; Red Line Editorial, 12, 40; Georgios Antonatos/Shutterstock Images, 17; Shutterstock Images, 19, 22, 32–33, 37, 43, 45; piemags/DCM/Alamy, 20; Wangkun Jia/Alamy, 24–25; Patsuda Paramee/Shutterstock Images, 27; Library of Congress/Corbis Historical/VCG/Getty Images, 28; Library of Congress, 30; Jaclyn Vernace/Shutterstock Images, 34; Joseph Prezioso/AFP/Getty Images, 35; Bill Uhrich/MediaNews Group/Reading Eagle/Getty Images, 38

Editors: Marie Pearson and Haley Williams
Series Designer: Ryan Gale

Library of Congress Control Number: 2023939622

Publisher's Cataloging-in-Publication Data
Names: Gagne, Tammy, author.
Title: The haunted history of Salem, Massachusetts / by Tammy Gagne
Description: Minneapolis, Minnesota: Abdo Publishing, 2024 | Series: Haunted history of the United States | Includes online resources and index.
Identifiers: ISBN 9781098292539 (lib. bdg.) | ISBN 9798384910473 (ebook)
Subjects: LCSH: Haunted places--United States--Juvenile literature. | History--Juvenile literature. | Ghosts--United States--Juvenile literature. | Salem (Mass.)--History--Juvenile literature.
Classification: DDC 133.109--dc23

CONTENTS

THE GHOSTS OF WITCH CITY

Sarah-Frankie Carter moved to Salem, Massachusetts, in 2008 and eventually became a tour guide. Her job involved leading visitors through some of the spookiest places in the historic city. But she was not working when she had one of the most frightening experiences of her life.

Carter and a friend were visiting the Howard Street Cemetery. She had heard stories about the ghost of one of the dead buried there. Giles Corey was accused of witchcraft in 1692. Knowing he could not be

Salem was originally known as Naumkeag, which is also the name of the American Indian peoples who first lived there.

Besides Giles Corey, five other men were found guilty of practicing witchcraft during the Salem witch trials.

tried for the crime unless he pleaded guilty or not guilty, he refused to do either. Corey died in a Salem field as the sheriff tortured him to get him to plead guilty. That field later became Howard Street Cemetery, which is next to the old Salem Jail.

Carter had a creepy feeling as she and her friend got closer to where Corey had been crushed to death.

Corey survived for three days as the sheriff placed more and more heavy rocks on top of his body. Some people who witnessed the event said that Corey had cried out "I curse you and Salem!" to the sheriff before taking his last breath.

Visitors to the graveyard have reported odd experiences. Some said they felt as if a heavy weight had been placed on their chests. Others said they saw the ghost of an elderly

CAN GHOSTS SHOW APPROVAL?

Rosemary Guiley has written many books about ghosts and witches. But in *Haunted Salem: Strange Phenomena in the Witch City*, she says there is an "energy of place that sets Salem apart, a brooding feeling that bridges the past to the present." She also shares that she encountered a ghost in Salem herself. While staying at a friend's home, Guiley heard a loud tapping sound in the middle of the night. She later came to believe it was the ghost of John Ropes, the house's first owner. The friend said the ghost made the noise only when he liked a guest. "I guess he approved of my research!" Guiley wrote.

man who walked around a tree in the cemetery. Many people think this man is the lingering spirit of Corey. Others have reported seeing a skeleton in old, ragged clothing. A legend states that if Corey appears this way, Salem will soon burn. The same legend warns that if the ghost speaks to the observers, they will die.

Carter's friend was trying to get a better look at the old jail when Carter heard her scream. The friend had seen something and thought it was Corey's ghost. Shortly after the encounter, Carter turned on her radio. A news story said that there were multiple fires burning in Salem.

SALEM'S FRIGHTFUL HISTORY

Salem is best known for the witch trials that happened in the early 1690s. Most people who lived in the small New England town at this time were known as Puritans. Puritans were members of an English Protestant

This statue depicts Roger Conant who, along with a group of settlers, founded Salem in 1626.

ROGER CONANT
BORN 1592 – DIED 1679
FIRST SETTLER OF SALEM 1626
a means, through grace assisting

The majority of those accused of witchcraft were women, with middle-aged and older women being accused more often.

religious group from the 1600s. Their religion upheld high standards for behavior. Actions such as swearing, lying, or fighting were swiftly punished, usually in public. Practicing witchcraft was punishable by death. The Puritans believed that witches were devil worshippers who had traded their souls to Satan for magical powers.

But while standards of behavior were high during that time, legal standards for finding people guilty of crimes were not. Courts pressured people accused of witchcraft into confessing. When people pleaded guilty, their lives were spared. Many of the people put to death in Salem refused to plead guilty. If two people claimed to have seen an act of witchcraft, their testimony led to a guilty verdict against the accused.

When a group of girls claimed that three women of the town were witches, the accused were put on trial. The girls claimed the women's spirits appeared to them in dreams while the women's bodies remained elsewhere. The court accepted this testimony, which it called spectral evidence.

In 1692, more than 200 people in Salem were accused of practicing witchcraft during the witch trials. By the year's end, 20 people had been found guilty of the

A GHOST WITH A TAIL

Many tourists stay at Salem's Daniels House, the city's oldest bed-and-breakfast, in hopes of encountering a four-legged ghost. This inn does not have a cat. Still, guests often tell the owner they have seen a gray-and-black striped cat roaming Daniels House. Some guests enjoy their encounters with the tiny ghost cat so much that they return in hopes of another visit from it. A few have even left a bowl of milk to attract the attention of the phantom feline.

SALEM'S MOST HAUNTED PLACES

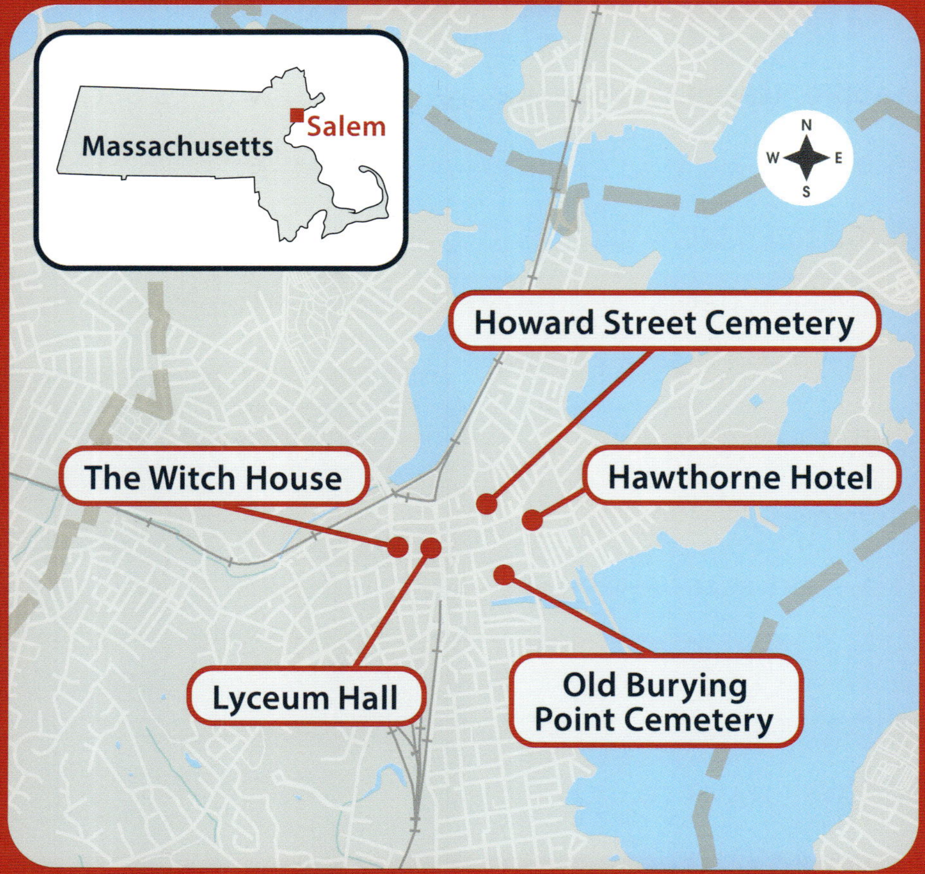

This map shows the locations of several areas believed to be haunted in Salem. Why do you think these supposedly haunted locations are so close to one another?

crime and put to death. Giles Corey was the only one crushed to death. The rest were hanged.

In 1957, the state officially apologized for the events that had occurred in Salem, which were by then regarded as a horrible mistake. But for many people, the city will always be linked to witches and ghosts. These historical events have turned Salem into a popular tourist destination. For example, in 2022, 2.2 million people visited Salem. Guides lead visitors on tours of the areas where the witch hysteria took place. Both tourists and locals have reported seeing ghosts in numerous parts of the city. The sites and their eerie histories have inspired ghost stories that are told all over the world.

EXPLORE ONLINE

Chapter One discusses the Salem witch trials of the early 1690s. The online article below goes into more detail on this topic. How is the information from the article the same as the information in Chapter One? What new information did you learn from the article?

THE SALEM WITCH TRIALS OF 1692
abdocorelibrary.com/haunted-salem-massachusetts

SPOOKY JUDGES

People have reported a variety of paranormal activity at the Witch House on Essex Street. The house belonged to Jonathan Corwin, one of the judges in the witch trials. Today, the home operates as a museum. It is the only original structure connected to the witch hysteria that is still standing in the city.

Both museum employees and visitors have reported seeing or hearing unusual things in the house. Some say they have seen strange shadows, while others have heard footsteps

Samuel Sewall was another notable judge during the Salem witch trials. He was the only judge to admit guilt for condemning those accused of witchcraft.

or whispers. Workers say the sounds happen most often when they are alone and closing for the day.

A television show featured the Witch House on one of its episodes in 2011. Zak Bagans and Nick Groff of *Ghost Adventures* were interviewing the house's director when strange things started happening. The batteries on Bagans's wireless microphone died. He quickly replaced them. But the new ones died immediately as well.

People can tour the Witch House and learn more about the Salem witch trials.

Groff told the *Boston Herald* he and the others think there was some sort of energy in the house that was draining the batteries.

The *Ghost Adventures* crew members also think they spoke with the ghost of Bridget Bishop. Bishop was the first person put to death during the witch trials. The team used electronic voice phenomenon (EVP) technology at the Witch House. The purpose of this software is to isolate sounds from ghosts in recordings. Ghost hunters say EVP can pick up sounds that human ears may not. The team asked the ghost who the person was who hanged them. A voice on the recording replied with what sounded like the name Mary. Mary Walcott was among the girls who accused Bishop of witchcraft.

OLD BURYING POINT CEMETERY

If there is any area where people might expect to see ghosts, it is a cemetery. The Old Burying Point Cemetery is also known as the Charter Street Cemetery. It is the oldest burying ground in Salem. One of

The Old Burying Point Cemetery was established in 1637. It is one of the oldest cemeteries in the United States.

the judges who ruled over the witch trials is buried

there. John Hathorne was nicknamed Hanging Judge

Hathorne because he sentenced so many people to

HERE LYES INTERD
y BODY OF COL IOHN
HATHORNE ESQR
AGED 76 YEARS
WHO DIED MAY y 10
1717

death by hanging. Hathorne was also Jonathan Corwin's brother-in-law.

Although Hathorne died in 1717, some people have reported seeing him more recently in Old Burying Point Cemetery. As with several other tourist attractions in Salem, many people visit the cemetery at night when it feels the spookiest. They often bring cameras and take photos of various graves. When some

MAKING A NAME FOR HIMSELF

Author Nathaniel Hawthorne was from Salem. He was the great-great grandson of John Hathorne. Hawthorne was ashamed of being related to the harsh judge of the witch trials. In fact, historians think that Hawthorne added the "w" to his last name so people wouldn't connect the two of them. One of Hawthorne's most famous novels is *The House of the Seven Gables*. He used Salem as the setting for the story. The family home that inspired the title is among the many places said to be haunted in Salem. Visitors can now tour the historic mansion, which still stands in the city.

John Hathorne was 76 years old when he died in 1717.

The gallows was a device used for executions by hanging.

visitors look at their pictures later, they notice a man near Hathorne's grave. Although he appears in the images, they claim they did not see him when they snapped the photos. Some people believe this is the ghost of the Hanging Judge because of his nearness to Hathorne's grave.

STRAIGHT TO THE
SOURCE

Sam Baltrusis visited many sites in Salem while writing his book *Ghosts of Salem: Haunts of the Witch City*. In his book, Baltrusis shares his impressions of the Witch House:

> *My favorite haunt in Salem is magistrate Jonathan Corwin's former home, also known as the Witch House. My assistant and I met with the director, Elizabeth Peterson, and walked around the only standing structure with ties to the witch trial hysteria of 1692. Trekking up the building's creaky stairs, it felt like we were stepping back in time. I swore I heard my name whispered on the first floor of the hallowed structure. The disembodied voice sounded female. My research assistant, a die-hard myth buster . . . thinks it was merely the power of suggestion.*

> Source: Sam Baltrusis. *Ghosts of Salem: Haunts of the Witch City.* History Press, 2014.

WHAT'S THE BIG IDEA?

Take a close look at this passage. How does Baltrusis's description of the Witch House make it sound as though it is haunted? What evidence does he provide to support his belief that it may indeed be haunted?

HAWTHORNE HOTEL AND THE LYCEUM

The Hawthorne Hotel has a long history in Salem. It was called the Archer Block when the building was first constructed in 1809. In 1818, it was renamed the Franklin Building. For more than 100 years, the Salem Marine Society used the building's rooms as lodging for sailors who came to the coastal town. But the Franklin Building was also known for tragedy. By 1860, the building had caught fire three times. The last of these blazes was the most disastrous. The entire structure had to be rebuilt. In 1921,

The Hawthorne Hotel has been a member of Historic Hotels of America since 1991.

AN AURA OF DISASTER

People who study paranormal activity think that fires can draw haunted energy to the sites of these destructive events. They say an "aura of disaster" can be left behind after a building burns. For this reason, some people believe the many fires at the Hawthorne Hotel site have made the building more prone to visits from ghosts.

the building was turned into a luxury hotel. Named after author Nathaniel Hawthorne, the Hawthorne Hotel has six stories and 150 rooms.

Yet another fire broke out at the hotel in 1997. The repeated fires made some people wonder if the site was cursed. Fires weren't the only reason for their suspicions. Over the years, guests and employees have reported seeing and hearing many scary things at the hotel. A ghostly woman is said to haunt room 612. Guests describe her as looking at her reflection in the mirror. Guests staying in room 325 have said they felt someone or something touching their hair or hands. Others have felt a tugging on their sheets. Guests in

other rooms have claimed to hear sinks running and toilets flushing on their own. One little boy was terrified by the sound of a child crying during the night, even though he and his mother were alone in their room.

The Salem Marine Society still occupies the top floor of the hotel. Employees say they sometimes arrive to find objects such as antique maps and charts scattered around the office. They say this happens despite locking up the items before leaving the previous day. Employees also report that the decorative ship's

Inventor Alexander Graham Bell gave a lecture at Lyceum Hall in 1877.

wheel on the top floor turns by itself. They say it is as if a sailor's ghost is at the helm. The female ghost from room 612 has also been said to wander the sixth floor.

LYCEUM HALL

Another Salem building that has served more than one purpose is Lyceum Hall. Built in 1831, the hall hosted lectures, author readings, and other forms of entertainment for many decades. Its famous speakers included Ralph Waldo Emerson, Oliver Wendell Holmes, and Henry David Thoreau. In 1692, however, the land was owned by the husband of Bridget Bishop. The Lyceum stands on the site of the orchard where Bishop grew apples.

In recent decades, different restaurants have occupied Lyceum Hall. More than once, some staff members have noticed upon returning to a room that furniture was not where it had

The Joshua Ward House is another location in Salem that many people believe is haunted.

been before. Others have repeatedly seen drinking glasses fly off shelves. Many of them think that Bridget Bishop's ghost is behind these strange occurrences. They have reported seeing a woman in a mirror across from a staircase. But the biggest reason they think the ghost is Bishop is because of the scent of apples that randomly seems to appear in the building.

STRAIGHT TO THE
SOURCE

Haunted Hotels in America author and travel historian Dr. Robin Mead thinks that Salem's history has had a long-lasting impact on the city as a whole:

> *The ghost of the Hawthorne Hotel is no single specter. It is in fact the all-pervading atmosphere of those grim days in the 1690s when Salem Common—and the land on which the Hawthorne Hotel now stands—was the focus of the dreadful witch hunts that raged through this, the oldest continuous Protestant society in America. . . .*
>
> *In the simple, God-fearing society of the time, any personal vanity, any simple pleasure such as dancing, any physical handicap, or even an irreverent sense of humor or a favorite pet, could be interpreted as an insult to the Lord. Cross your neighbor and you could find yourself denounced as consorting with Satan.*
>
> Source: Robin Mead. *Haunted Hotels in America.*
> Thomas Nelson, 2022.

CONSIDER YOUR AUDIENCE

Read the passage above closely. Write a blog post about this information for a new audience, such as your classmates. How does your post differ from the original text, and why?

SALEM WITCH MUSEUM

CHAPTER
FOUR

ARE SALEM'S GHOSTS REAL?

For a long time, many people in Salem were embarrassed by the witch trials from the city's past. But people who believed in witchcraft were drawn to the city. While some residents still tried to put the past behind them, others started embracing the city's history in the 1970s. They quickly learned that the Witch City image helped tourism tremendously.

Salem's police cars now display images of witches riding brooms. A Salem public elementary school is named Witchcraft Heights. The city's high school sports teams

The Salem Witch Museum is one of many popular tourist attractions in Salem.

call themselves the Salem Witches. Even the newspaper,
the *Salem News*, features an image of a witch next to
its title.

In recent decades, ghost hunters have become
fascinated with Salem. While many of these people
search for ghosts just for fun, others do it as a job.
Several television shows work to prove or disprove
stories about hauntings. In 2007, the team from the
show *Ghost Hunters* visited Salem to investigate
common reports of hauntings at the Hawthorne Hotel
and the restaurant at Lyceum Hall. Although the team

The Official Salem Witches' Halloween Ball is held every year in Salem to celebrate magic and to honor the dead.

saw no ghosts at either location, it did uncover potential explanations for some of the reported hauntings.

At the hotel, the *Ghost Hunters* team heard what guests have described as bathroom sinks turning on by themselves. But the team found that the sound was coming from other areas of the hotel. Team members could hear the sound as it moved through pipes inside

LOOKING TO SCIENCE FOR ANSWERS

Some of the most common types of paranormal activity that people report involve quick temperature drops or cold breezes. While some people think these are signs of a ghost's presence, there are also scientific explanations for those kinds of changes. The simplest explanation is drafts. Many buildings have currents of air that go through them. They are especially common in old houses, which often have poor insulation. Hot air rises while cold air falls. These natural movements can lead people to believe that a ghost has moved past them.

the building's thin walls. They also found an explanation for the ghost seen in the mirror at the restaurant. The *Ghost Hunters* team noticed that when cars drove by the building at night, their headlights reflected off several mirrors in the establishment. The mirror in which the ghost was seen had an uneven surface. The result was brief images of light that a person could easily mistake for

People's brains can sometimes misinterpret what they see in a mirror, so they might think they're seeing a ghost.

Ghost hunters use a variety of equipment, such as infrared cameras and audio recorders, to search for evidence of ghosts.

a ghost moving on the stairs. While the team could not say for sure that either location isn't haunted, it also did not find any evidence of a haunting.

OTHER EXPLANATIONS

Other claims of hauntings have been explained too. Some visitors to Salem's Witch Dungeon Museum believed they saw a rocking chair move on its own in the building. But the museum's founder disproved this himself. He blamed the movement on a cat that wandered in and out of the building. When the animal bumped the chair, it rocked back and forth. In the low light of the museum tour, it was easy for visitors to miss the feline trespasser.

The abundance of ghost stories about Salem may explain some of the spooky experiences people keep having in the city. Studies show that people are more

PERSPECTIVES

TOURIST TRAP

Margaret Press is an author who lives in Salem. Press doesn't believe the city is haunted by ghosts of previous residents. She thinks that Salem's tourism groups are what keep visitors' beliefs in the city's ghosts alive. She also worries that focusing so much on witches and hauntings teaches young people to believe in ghost stories over science. Press points out, "Salem makes it easy for us to find these patterns because of historic accident. It's not in the ground. It's not in the air. It's in ourselves."

TRUE BELIEVERS

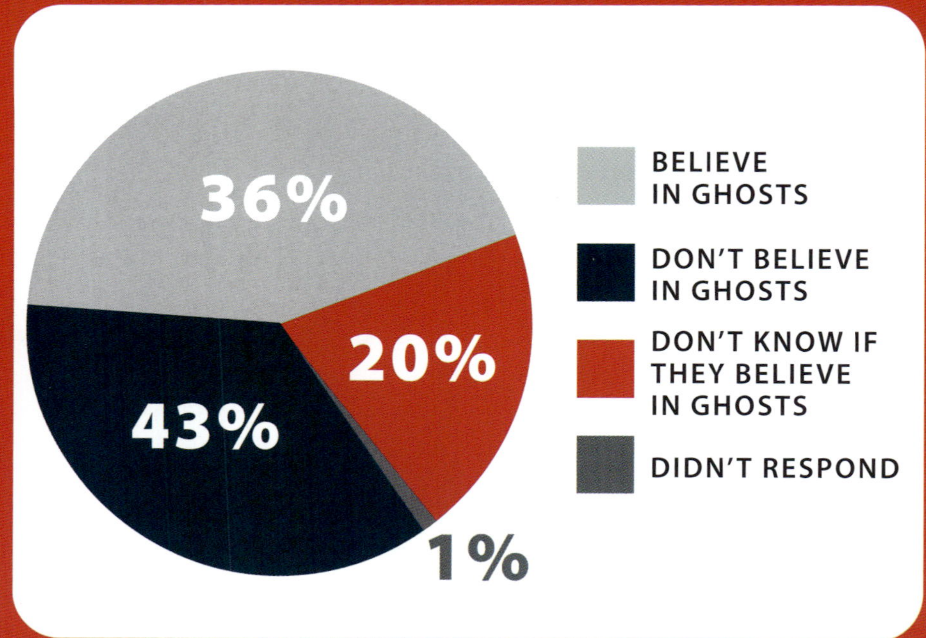

According to a 2021 poll by Statista, more than one-third of the American population believe ghosts exist. How does this information help you understand the importance of Salem in American society?

likely to think they have witnessed a paranormal event if others have already made similar claims. In one such study, two groups of subjects toured a theater. Only one group was told that the theater was said to be haunted. More people in that group reported paranormal experiences during the tour. Some people think this could be what happens to Salem's visitors and residents.

No one has been able to prove whether ghosts exist. Many reports of paranormal activity in Salem have yet to be explained by anyone. But one thing is certain. Salem has plenty of haunted history to fascinate even the biggest disbelievers.

FURTHER EVIDENCE

Chapter Four discusses the debate over whether ghosts are indeed real. What is the main idea of this chapter? What key evidence supports this idea? Take a look at the website below. Find information from the site that supports the main idea of the chapter. Does the information support an existing piece of evidence in the chapter, or does it add new evidence?

ARE GHOSTS REAL?

abdocorelibrary.com/haunted-salem-massachusetts

FAST FACTS

- In the early 1690s, the town of Salem, Massachusetts, held a series of witch trials. Twenty people were put to death for the crime of witchcraft.

- One of the people accused of witchcraft was a man named Giles Corey. Some people claim they have seen his ghost in the Howard Street Cemetery.

- The home of witch trials judge Jonathan Corwin is also said to be haunted. The show *Ghost Adventures* featured the house in 2011.

- Guests at Salem's Hawthorne Hotel have had a variety of odd experiences. They have reported seeing ghosts and hearing disembodied voices.

- The ghost of Bridget Bishop, the first person executed for witchcraft in Salem, is said to fill Lyceum Hall with the scent of apples. This building now stands where her family's apple orchard once grew.

- Many ghost hunters have visited Salem. They have tried to prove or disprove the existence of ghosts and hauntings.

- Some people believe much of the city of Salem is haunted. Others think there are more scientific explanations for the experiences people have claimed to have in the city.

Dig Deeper

After reading this book, what questions do you still have about Salem, Massachusetts? With an adult's help, find a few reliable sources that can help you answer your questions. Write a paragraph about what you learned.

Surprise Me

This book discusses the witchcraft trials of the early 1690s. After reading this book, what two or three facts about this part of the city's history did you find most surprising? Write a few sentences about each one. Why did you find them surprising?

You Are There

This book talks about ghosts people have claimed to have seen in Salem's cemeteries. Imagine that you are taking a tour of the city and see or hear something unexpected in one of the city's graveyards. Write a letter to a friend or family member describing the event. Be sure to add plenty of details.

Another View

This book discusses many accounts of hauntings in Salem. As you know, every source is different. Ask a librarian or another adult to help you find a second source about one of these events. Write a short essay comparing and contrasting the new source's point of view with that of this book's author. What is the point of view of each author? How are they similar and why? How are they different and why?

GLOSSARY

aura
an energy field that
surrounds a certain area

condemning
sentencing someone to
a particular punishment,
especially death

disembodied
not connected to a body

hysteria
behavior marked by
overwhelming fear

infrared
a type of light that is not
visible to the human eye

irreverent
lacking respect

paranormal
events that can't be
explained by science

phantom
a ghost or an imagined figure

spectral
like a ghost or from a ghost

ONLINE RESOURCES

To learn more about hauntings and Salem, Massachusetts, visit our free resource websites below.

Visit **abdocorelibrary.com** or scan this QR code for free Common Core resources for teachers and students, including vetted activities, multimedia, and booklinks, for deeper subject comprehension.

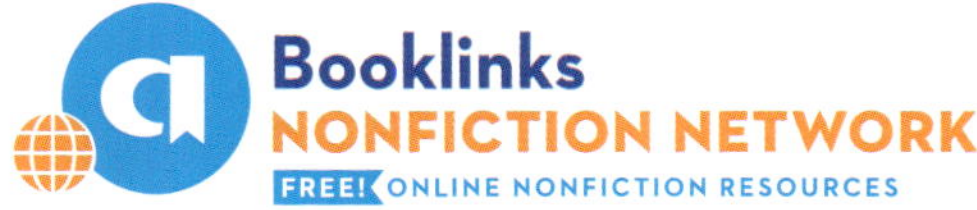

Visit **abdobooklinks.com** or scan this QR code for free additional online weblinks for further learning. These links are routinely monitored and updated to provide the most current information available.

LEARN MORE

Hamilton, S. L. *The World's Most Ghoulish Ghosts*. Abdo, 2022.

Mooney, Carla. *Hauntings*. BrightPoint Press, 2024.

Reynolds, Donna. *The Salem Witch Trials*. Cavendish Square, 2021.

INDEX

About the Author

Tammy Gagne is an author and editor who specializes in nonfiction. She has written hundreds of books for both children and adults. She lives in northern New England with her husband, son, and dogs.